Latin So American Fish Recipes

Gain creativity, tastefulness and a perfect weight balance, with these mouth-watering, quick and easy recipes for beginners. Seduce your partner and amaze your meals. This cookbook will also run you into a healthy and detox-based lifestyle, for a body and mind energy boost

Ernest Pescara

Table of Contents

Welcome, dear!

This is my offer to your cooking style.

This cookbook is the realization of my research on how to eat tasty and healthy food at the meantime.
My purpose is to increase your energies and to let you live a lighter life, without the junk of the globalised kitchen.

In here, you'll find my knowledge on how to create delicious dishes with South American fishes.

Jump into a worldwide discovery of good food and natural-feed animals, with many recipes for a varied diet.

Nevertheless, you'll learn new techniques, discover tastes of all around the world and improve your skills.
Let yourself be inspired by the worldwide traditions, twisted by a proper chef.

Each of these dishes is thought to:

1 – Let you understand how to work with South American fish

This majestic animal is presented in various dishes of different cultures, to show you how the same ingredient can change from dish to dish.

2 – Balance your weight with different cooking methods

As soon as you learn different ways to cook your fish, you'll discover an entire world of new ideas.

South American fish will never bore you again!

3 – Amaze your friends starting from the smell

Once your friends will come to dinner, they will be in love with your food even before to see your creation.

South American Fish Recipes

Grilled Tuna Steaks

Serves 4 pax

Ingredients

- 1 plum tomato, cored, seeded, and chopped
- 1 slice hearty white sandwich bread, crusts removed, bread lightly toasted and cut into 1/2-inch pieces
- 1 teaspoon water
- 2 tablespoons slivered almonds, toasted
- 4 (8- to 12-ounce) skinless tuna steaks, 1 inch thick, halved crosswise
- 3 teaspoons honey
- 1/8 teaspoon cayenne pepper
- 1/4 cup extra-virgin olive oil
- 1 cup jarred roasted red peppers, rinsed, patted dry, and chopped coarse
- 1 garlic clove, minced
- 2 teaspoons sherry vinegar
- Salt and pepper

Procedure

1. Process bread and almonds using a food processor until nuts are finely ground, 10 to 15 seconds. Put in red peppers, tomato, 1 tablespoon oil, vinegar, garlic, cayenne, and 1/2 teaspoon salt.

2. Process until smooth and mixture has texture similar to mayonnaise, 20 to 30 seconds, scraping down sides of the container as required. Sprinkle with salt to taste; set aside for serving.

3. Beat remaining 3 tablespoons oil, honey, water, 1/2 teaspoon salt, and pinch pepper together in a container. Pat tuna dry using paper towels and heavily brush with oil mixture.

4. FOR A GAS GRILL Turn all burners to high, cover, and heat grill until hot, about fifteen minutes. Leave all burners on high.

5. Clean cooking grate, then repetitively brush grate with thoroughly oiled paper towels until grate is black and glossy, 5 to 10 times.

6. Place tuna on grill (on hotter side if using charcoal) and cook (covered if using gas) until opaque and streaked with dark grill marks on first side, 1 to 3 minutes.

7. Gently flip tuna using 2 spatulas and carry on cooking until opaque at perimeter and translucent red at center when checked with tip of paring knife and registers 110 degrees (for rare), about 2 minutes, or until opaque at perimeter and reddish pink at center when checked with tip of paring knife and registers 125 degrees (for medium-rare), approximately three minutes. Serve with sauce.

Fish Tacos and Sour Vegs

Ingredients

- 1 cup fresh cilantro leaves
- 1 cup Mexican crema
- 1 quart peanut or vegetable oil
- 1/4 cup cornstarch
- 3/4 cup all purpose flour
- 1 cup beer
- 6 pounds skinless whitefish fillets, such as cod, haddock, or halibut, cut crosswise into 4 by an inch strips
- Salt and pepper
- 1 recipe Pickled Onion and Cabbage
- 1 teaspoon baking powder
- 18 x 6 inches corn tortillas, warmed

Procedure

1. Adjust oven rack to middle position and heat oven to 200 degrees. Set wire rack in rimmed baking sheet. Pat fish dry using paper towels and sprinkle with salt and pepper.

2. Whisk flour, cornstarch, baking powder, and 1 teaspoon salt together in big container. Put in beer and whisk until the desired smoothness is achieved. Put in fish to batter and toss to coat uniformly.

3. Put in oil to big Dutch oven until it measures about 3/4 inch deep and heat over moderate high heat to 350 degrees.

4. Remove five or six pieces of fish from batter, allowing surplus to drip back into container, and put into hot oil, for a short period of time dragging fish along surface of oil to stop sticking.

5. Adjust burner, if required, to maintain oil temperature between 325 and 350 degrees. Fry fish, stirring slowly to stop pieces from clinging together and turning as required, until a golden-brown color is achieved and crunchy, approximately eight minutes.

6. Move fish to readied wire rack and place in oven to keep warm. Return oil to 350 degrees and repeat with the rest of the fish, working with five or six pieces at a time.

7. Serve with warm tortillas, cilantro, crema, and Pickled Onion and Cabbage.

Searing Shrimp

Serves 8 pax

Ingredients

- 1 bay leaf
- 31 pounds medium-large shrimp
- 1 tablespoon minced parsley
- 1/4 teaspoon salt
- 1/2 cup extra-virgin olive oil
- 2 inches) piece mild dried chile, approximately broken, with seeds
- 2 teaspoons sherry vinegar
- 14 garlic cloves, peeled, 2 cloves minced, 12 cloves left whole

Procedure

1. Toss shrimp with minced garlic, 2 tablespoons oil, and salt in a container and allow to marinate at room temperature for minimum half an hour or maximum 1 hour.

2. In the meantime, use the flat side of a chef's knife to smash 4 garlic cloves. Heat smashed garlic and remaining 6 tablespoons oil in 12-inch frying pan over moderate to low heat, stirring intermittently, until garlic is light golden brown, four to eight minutes; allow the oil to cool to room temperature. Using slotted spoon, take out and discard smashed garlic.

3. Finely cut remaining 8 garlic cloves. Return frying pan with cooled oil to low heat and put in sliced garlic, bay leaf, and chile. Cook, stirring intermittently, until garlic becomes soft but not browned, four to eight minutes. If garlic does not begin to sizzle after 3 minutes, raise the heat to moderate to low.

4. Increase heat to moderate to low and put in shrimp with marinade. Cook, without stirring, until oil starts to bubble mildly, approximately two minutes.
5. Using tongs, flip shrimp and carry on cooking until almost cooked through, approximately two minutes. Increase heat to high and put in vinegar and parsley.
6. Cook, stirring continuously, until shrimp are cooked through and oil is bubbling heavily, 15 to 20 seconds.
7. Take out and throw away the bay leaf. Serve instantly.

Braised Halibut

Ingredients

- 1 teaspoon Dijon mustard
- 4 (4- to 6-ounce) skinless halibut fillets, 3/4 to 1 inch thick
- Lemon wedges
- 1/4 cup extra-virgin olive oil, plus extra for serving
- 3/4 cup dry white wine
- 1 pound leeks, white and light green parts only, halved along the length, sliced thin, and washed thoroughly
- 1 tablespoon minced fresh parsley
- Salt and pepper

Procedure

1. Pat halibut dry using paper towels and drizzle with 1/2 teaspoon salt. Heat oil in 12-inch frying pan on moderate heat until warm, approximately fifteen seconds.

2. Place halibut skinned side up in frying pan and cook until bottom half of halibut begins to turn opaque (halibut should not brown), about 4 minutes. Cautiously move halibut raw side down to large plate.

3. Put in leeks, mustard, and 1/4 teaspoon salt to oil left in frying pan and cook on moderate heat, stirring often, till they become tender, 10 to 12 minutes. Mix in wine and bring to simmer.

4. Place halibut raw side down on top of leeks. Decrease heat to moderate to low, cover, and simmer gently until halibut flakes apart when softly poked using paring knife and registers 140 degrees, 6 to 10 minutes.

5. Cautiously move halibut to serving platter, tent loosely with aluminium foil, and allow to rest while finishing leeks.

6. Return leeks to high heat and simmer briskly until mixture becomes thick slightly, 2 to 4 minutes.

7. Sprinkle with salt and pepper to taste. Arrange leek mixture around halibut, drizzle with extra oil, and drizzle with parsley.

8. Serve with lemon wedges.

Broiled Grouper Wrap

Serves 4 pax

Ingredients

- 1 (16-ounce) jar grape leaves
- 1 tablespoon capers, rinsed and minced
- 1 teaspoon grated lemon zest
- 1/2 cup Tahini-Lemon Dressing
- 1/2 teaspoon pepper
- 1/2 teaspoon salt
- 3 tablespoons minced fresh parsley
- 5 tablespoons extra-virgin olive oil, plus extra for brushing
- 4 (4- to 6-ounce) skinless grouper fillets, 3/4 to 1 inch thick

Procedure

1. Beat oil, parsley, capers, lemon zest, salt, and pepper together in medium bowl. Put in grouper and gently turn to coat. Cover and put in the fridge while preparing grape leaves.

2. Reserve 24 undamaged grape leaves, approximately 6 inches in diameter; save for later rest of the leaves for another use. Bring 8 cups water to boil in a big saucepan. Put in grape leaves and cook for about five minutes.

3. Gently drain leaves and move to a container of cold water to cool, approximately five minutes. Drain again thoroughly.

4. Place oven rack 8 inches from broiler element and heat broiler. Set wire rack in rimmed baking sheet and spray using vegetable oil spray. Shingle 5 leaves smooth side down on counter into 9-inch circle with stems pointing toward center of circle, then place 1 leaf smooth side down over opening in center.

5. Place 1 fillet in center of leaf circle and spoon portion of remaining marinade on top. Fold sides of leaf circle over grouper, then fold up bottom of circle and continue to roll tightly into packet.

6. Move packet seam side down to prepared rack. Replicate the process with the rest of the grape leaves, fillets, and marinade.

7. Pat tops of grouper packets dry using paper towels and brush with extra oil. Broil until grape leaves are crisp and mildly charred and grouper registers 140 degrees, 12 to 18 minutes, rotating sheet halfway through broiling.

8. Serve with Tahini Lemon Dressing.

Easy-Roasted Halibut with Chermoula

Serves 8 pax

Ingredients

For the Chermoula:

- 1/8 teaspoon cayenne pepper
- 3/4 cup fresh cilantro leaves
- 2 tablespoons lemon juice
- 4 garlic cloves, minced
- 1/4 cup extra-virgin olive oil
- 1/4 teaspoon salt
- 1/2 teaspoon ground cumin
- 1/2 teaspoon paprika

For the Fish:

- 2 tablespoons extra-virgin olive oil
- 2 (11/4-pound) skin-on full halibut steaks, 1 inch thick and 10 to 12 inches long, trimmed
- Salt and pepper

Procedure

For the Chermoula:

1. Process all ingredients using a food processor until smooth, approximately one minute, scraping down sides of the container as required; set aside for serving.

For the Fish:

2. Place the oven rack in the centre of the oven and pre-heat your oven to 325 degrees. Pat halibut dry using paper towels and sprinkle with salt and pepper.
3. Heat oil in 12-inch oven-safe non-stick frying pan on moderate to high heat until just smoking. Place halibut in frying pan and cook until thoroughly browned on first side, approximately five minutes.
4. Gently flip halibut using 2 spatulas and move frying pan to oven.
5. Roast until halibut flakes apart when softly poked using paring knife and registers 140 degrees, 6 to 9 minutes.

6. Cautiously move halibut to slicing board, tent loosely with aluminium foil, and allow to rest for about five minutes.
7. Remove skin from steaks and separate each quadrant of meat from bones by slipping knife or spatula between them.
8. Serve with chermoula.

Carp Caviar

Serves 6 pax

Ingredients

- 1/4 cup vegetable or olive oil
- 3 tablespoons finely chopped white onion
- About 6 ounces tomatoes, finely chopped
- 1 garlic clove, finely chopped
- 1 pound carp roe
- 1 tablespoon salt

The toppings

- 1/3 cup finely chopped cilantro
- 1/3 cup finely chopped serrano chiles or any other fresh, hot green chiles
- 1/3 cup finely chopped green, unripe tomatoes
- 1/2 cup finely chopped white onion

Procedure

1. Place the salt and enough water to cover the roe in a shallow pan and bring to the simmering point. Put in the roe and allow it to simmer for eight to ten minutes, depending on thickness, then remove and drain.

2. When it is sufficiently cool to handle, take off the skin and crumble the roe.

3. Heat the oil in a heavy pan. Put in the tomatoes, onion, and garlic and fry over quite high heat while stirring occasionally and scraping the bottom of the pan, until the onion is tender and the mixture is almost dry.

4. Put in the crumbled roe with salt to taste and carry on frying the mixture on moderate heat, flipping it over continuously, until dry and crumbly, approximately five minutes.

5. Serve hot, accompanied by the onion and the other finely chopped toppings, in small different bowls, and a pile of hot corn tortillas.

Seafood Cocktail

Serves 6 pax

Ingredients

- 2 heaped tablespoons finely chopped cilantro
- A dozen big raw clams or scallops or medium-size cooked shrimps
- 3 tablespoons olive oil
- 4 serrano chiles or any fresh, hot green chiles, finely chopped with seeds
- 1/2 cup fresh lime juice
- 1 big avocado, cubed
- 1 small white onion, finely chopped
- About 12 ounces tomatoes, finely chopped
- Salt and freshly ground pepper to taste

Procedure

1. If you are using clams, open them or have them opened for you, saving both the clams and their juice.

2. If you are using scallops, allow them to marinate in the lime juice for about 1 hour or so.

3. Mix the clams (and their liquid) or other seafood with the remaining ingredients, tweak the seasoning, and serve slightly chilled.

Fish Tacos

Ingredients

- 1 red bell pepper, stemmed, seeded, and sliced
- 2 pounds skinless swordfish steaks, an inch thick, cut
- 2 tablespoons minced fresh cilantro
- 2 tablespoons tomato paste
- 1 tablespoon ancho chile powder
- 1 teaspoon dried oregano
- 1 teaspoon ground coriander
- 18 x 6 inches corn tortillas
- 1/2 cup orange juice
- 1 jalapeño chile
- 1 pineapple, peeled, quartered along the length
- 2 garlic cloves, minced
- 3 teaspoons chipotle chile powder
- 5 tablespoons vegetable oil
- 6 tablespoons lime juice
- Salt

Procedure

1. Heat 2 tablespoons oil, ancho chile powder, and chipotle chile powder in 8 inches

2. frying pan on moderate heat, stirring continuously, until aromatic and some bubbles form, two to three minutes.

3. Put in garlic, oregano, coriander, and 1 teaspoon salt and carry on cooking until aromatic, approximately half a minute. Put in tomato paste and, using spatula, purée tomato paste with spice mixture until blended, approximately twenty seconds.

4. Mix in orange juice and 2 tablespoons lime juice. Cook while stirring continuously, until meticulously mixed and reduced slightly, approximately 2 minutes. Move chile mixture to big container and allow to cool for fifteen minutes.

5. Put in swordfish to chile mixture and stir slowly to coat. Cover and place in your fridge for minimum 30 minutes or maximum 2 hours. Brush pineapple and jalapeño with remaining 1 tablespoon oil.

6. **For A Gas Grill:** Set all burners to high, cover, and heat grill until hot, approximately fifteen minutes. Turn all burners to moderate high.

7. Clean and oil cooking grate. Put fish, pineapple, and jalapeño on grill. Cover and cook until fish, pineapple, and jalapeño have begun to brown, three to five minutes.

8. Using thin spatula, turn fish, pineapple, and jalapeño. Cover and cook until pineapple and jalapeño are thoroughly browned and swordfish records 140 degrees, three to five minutes; move to platter and cover using aluminium foil.

9. Working in batches, grill tortillas, turning as required, until warm and soft, approximately half a minute; wrap firmly in foil to keep tender.

10. Chop pineapple and jalapeño fine and mix with bell pepper, cilantro, and remaining 4 tablespoons lime juice in container.

11. Sprinkle with salt to taste. Using 2 forks, pull fish apart into big flakes and serve with pineapple salsa and tortillas.

Crab and Tomatoes Spicy Broth

Serves 6 pax

Ingredients

- 6 cups boiling, salted water
- 12 live female crabs
- 2 jalapeño chiles, broiled
- 2 big sprigs epazote
- 3 tablespoons olive oil
- 1/2 big white onion, thickly cut and broiled
- 1 ancho chile, seeds and veins removed
- 1 pound tomatoes, broiled
- 6 garlic cloves, broiled and peeled

Procedure

1. If you dare, scrub the crabs well in cold water, and drop them into the pan with the boiling water. Allow them to cook for no more than three minutes. Remove all but 2 of the crabs and allow to cool. Boil the rest of the crabs for about ten minutes, then discard them.

2. When sufficiently cool to handle, remove the bell-shaped piece of the shell, and pry off the back shell. Scrape out the orange eggs, if any, and pry out any fat lurking in the extreme points of the shell and reserve in a small container.

3. Take away the spongy gills and grind them until a paste is achieved with the eggs and fat in a molcajete or blender. Reserve.

4. Cut each crab in half and crack the claws. Reserve. Return the shells and debris to the pan and allow them to simmer for approximately ten minutes.

5. Strain the broth through a twofold thickness of cheesecloth and return to the pan, discarding all the debris. There must be about 5 cups broth. If not, put in water to make up to that amount.

6. Put 1 cup of the reserved crab broth into your blender jar, put in the ancho chile pieces, onion, garlic, tomatoes, and chiles, and blend to a slightly textured consistency.

7. Heat the oil in a frying pan and fry the sauce using high heat, stirring occasionally to prevent sticking, until reduced and seasoned—about five minutes.

8. Put into the broth in the pan and simmer for approximately five minutes. Put in the paste of fat and eggs and simmer for a few minutes more.

9. Then put in the crabs, including the claws, and epazote and simmer again for yet another five minutes.

10. Serve in deep bowls with French bread or rolls.

Broiled Chili Fish

Serves 6 pax

Ingredients

- 5 tablespoons vegetable oil
- 3 ancho chiles, seeds and veins removed
- 1/2 cup mild vinegar
- 1 4-pound (1.8-kg) red snapper or grouper, gutted but scales, head, and tail left on 2 teaspoons salt, or to taste
- 3 garlic cloves
- 2 piquín chiles, left whole

Procedure

1. Cover the ancho chiles with boiling water and allow them to soak until soft—about five minutes. Drain the chiles, then move to a blender jar.

2. Put in the piquín chiles (whole), garlic, salt, and vinegar and blend until the desired smoothness is achieved. (the mixture must be like a thick paste. If any more liquid is needed to release the blades of the blender, use a minimum amount of water.)

3. Broil the fish for a short period of time on both sides, unseasoned, and strip off the skin.

4. Spread the outside of the fish with the chile paste, then coat with the oil and broil until thoroughly cooked—ten to fifteen minutes on each side depending on the thickness of the fish.

5. Serve instantly, with hot, freshly made tortillas.

Green Sauced Fish

Serves 6 pax

Ingredients

- 1/2 teaspoon salt
- 1/4 teaspoon cumin seeds
- 1/4 teaspoon peppercorns
- 2 pounds Juice of 1 big pompano lime
- 1/8 teaspoon dried mexican oregano
- 1/3 cup olive oil
- 1/3 cup water
- 1/2 green pepper, seeds and veins removed, chopped
- 1 pound green (unripe) tomatoes, roughly chopped
- 2 sprigs fresh cilantro, roughly chopped
- 3 scallions, roughly chopped
- Salt to taste
- 1 serrano chile, roughly chopped
- 1 tablespoon mild white vinegar
- 2 garlic cloves, roughly chopped
- 2 sprigs flat-leaf parsley, roughly chopped

Procedure

1. Have the fish cleaned, leaving the heads and tails on.
2. Grind the spices together dry and mix with the lime juice.
3. Prick the fish all over with a coarse-tined fork and rub the seasoning in well. Set aside, in an ovenproof dish, to season for minimum 1/2 hour.
4. Preheat your oven to 300° f (150° c).
5. Place the water and vinegar into your blender jar and put in the sauce ingredients apart from the oil a little at a time, blending after each addition until you have a slightly textured mixture.
6. Place a little of the oil under the fish, pour the sauce over the fish with the remaining oil, and bake, loosely covered, for approximately twenty minutes.
7. Turn the fish over cautiously and bake for another fifteen minutes, coating with the sauce occasionally.

Raw Sour Fish

Serves 6 pax

Ingredients

- 1 pound skinned fillets of sierra (kingfish)
- 12 ounces tomatoes, finely chopped
- 4 canned serrano chiles en escabeche
- 1/4 cup olive oil
- 1/2 teaspoon dried mexican oregano
- 1/2 teaspoon salt, or to taste
- Freshly ground pepper
- Juice of 6 or 7 big limes, diluted with approximately 1/2 cup water

For the serving:

- 1 small purple onion, cut into rings
- 1 small avocado, cut
- 2 tablespoons chopped cilantro

Procedure

1. Chop the fish into little cubes, approximately 1/2 inch, and cover them with the lime juice.
2. Set the fish aside on the bottom of the fridge until the fish loses its transparent look and becomes opaque, approximately three hours.
3. Mix the pieces occasionally so that they get uniformly "cooked" in the lime juice.
4. Put in the tomatoes with the remaining ingredients.
5. Set the ceviche aside on the bottom of the fridge for minimum 1 hour to season. (you should serve it chilled, but not so cold that the oil congeals.)
6. Before you serve, top each portion with slices of avocado and onion rings and drizzle with a little chopped cilantro, if you wish. Best eaten the same day.

Argentina Snapper

Ingredients

- 1/4 cup plus 3 tablespoons olive oil
- 12 pitted green olives or stuffed with red pepper, cut
- 2 big garlic cloves, cut
- 2 jalapeño chiles en escabeche, cut into strips
- 1/4 teaspoon dried mexican oregano
- 1/2 teaspoon salt, or to taste
- 1 cup thinly cut white onion
- 1 teaspoon salt, or to taste
- 2 tablespoons fresh lime juice
- A 3-pound red snapper
- 2mexican bay leaves
- 12 pounds tomatoes, finely chopped
- 3 tablespoons big capers

Procedure

1. Preheat your oven to 325° f.

2. Have the fish cleaned, leaving the head and tail on. Prick the fish on both sides with a coarse-tined fork, rub in the salt and lime juice, and set it aside in an ovenproof dish to season for approximately 2 hours.

3. Heat 1/4 cup oil in a frying pan and fry the onion and garlic, without browning, until they are tender. Put in the tomatoes, with the remaining ingredients, to the pan and cook the sauce over brisk heat until it is well seasoned and some of the juice has vaporized—about ten minutes. Pour the sauce over the fish.

4. Drizzle the rest of the 3 tablespoons oil over the sauce and bake the fish for approximately twenty minutes, loosely covered, on one side.

5. Turn the fish over very cautiously and carry on baking it until it is just soft—about twenty minutes.

6. Baste the fish regularly with the sauce during the cooking time.

Mexican Sauced Fish

Ingredients

- 2 cups water
- 1/2 cup vegetable oil
- 4 cups thinly cut purple onions, blanched
- 2 güero chiles, toasted but not skinned
- 1/4 cup fresh lime juice
- 1 cup water
- 1/2 cup wine vinegar
- 1/2 teaspoon coriander seeds, crushed
- 1/2 teaspoon cumin seeds, crushed
- 1/2 teaspoon dried mexican oregano
- 1/2 teaspoon granulated sugar
- 1 teaspoon salt
- 1-inch- thick steaks of sierra or salmon
- 1/2 cup water
- 1/2 teaspoon peppercorns, crushed
- 1/2-inch piece of cinnamon stick, broken up

- 10 small garlic cloves, toasted, peeled and left whole
- 2 mexican bay leaves
- 1 tsp whole allspice, crushed
- Salt to taste
- 1/2 cup olive oil
- 3/4 cup wine vinegar

Procedure

1. Pour the water, lime juice, and salt over the fish and set it aside for an hour, turning it once during that time.
2. Pulverize the spices in an electric grinder or mortar. Crush the 2 garlic cloves and grind them until a paste is achieved with the spices.
3. Place the spice-garlic paste into the deep cooking pan with the remaining ingredients in step 1 and bring the mixture to its boiling point.

4. Put in the oil, vinegar, and water and once again bring the mixture to its boiling point. Set aside and keep hot.

5. Dry the fish slices meticulously. Heat the oil in a frying pan and fry them about five minutes on each side. They must be barely cooked. Put them in a serving dish and pour the hot souse over them. Put in the chiles and onions. Set the fish aside to season for minimum 1 hour in the souse.

6. Serve at room temperature.

Stuffed Crabs

Serves 6 pax

Ingredients

- 2 tablespoons salt
- 2 tablespoons thoroughly ground, toasted breadcrumbs
- 8 big blue crabs
- 12 ounces tomatoes, finely chopped
- 1/4 cup plus 3 tablespoons olive oil
- 1/2 teaspoon salt, or to taste
- 2/3 cup finely chopped white onion
- 1 garlic clove, finely chopped
- 2 tablespoons big capers, washed
- 2 tablespoons finely chopped flat-leaf parsley
- 2 serrano chiles, finely chopped

Procedure

1. Drop the crabs into boiling, salted water and cover the deep cooking pan. Bring them to its boiling point and cook them for approximately 3 minutes. Remove and drain.

2. When they are sufficiently cool to handle, remove the heart-shaped breastplate and pry off the big back shell, keeping it undamaged.

3. Scrape out any fat and eggs that have remained in the shell, as well as those in the crab itself. Set them aside.

4. Scrub 6 of the shells well and set them aside. Take away the meat from the crabs and set it aside. Preheat your oven to 350° f.

5. Heat the 1/4 cup olive oil in a frying pan and fry the garlic and onion until they barely start to turn golden.

6. Put in the tomatoes, parsley, chiles, capers, and salt, and cook the mixture over a moderate heat until it is almost dry—5 to 8 minutes.

7. Mix in the crabmeat and take out of the heat.

8. Fill the crab shells with the crabmeat mixture, drizzle with the breadcrumbs and remaining 3 tablespoons olive oil and put the shells in your oven just long enough to heat them through.

9. Turn on the broiler and brown the surface of the stuffing.

Roasted Amarillo Cod

Ingredients

- 1/2 teaspoon sugar
- 1 (8 ounce) bottle clam broth
- 1 onion, chopped
- 5 tablespoons vegetable oil
- 2 guajillo chiles, stemmed, seeded, and torn
- 2 garlic cloves, peeled
- 3 sprigs cilantro
- 8 ounces tomatillos, husks and stems removed, washed well, dried, and slice into 1/2 inch pieces
- 1/8 teaspoon ground allspice
- 1/8 teaspoon ground cloves
- 1/4 teaspoon whole cumin seeds
- 1/2 teaspoon dried oregano
- 2 tablespoons masa harina
- 4 (6 to 8 ounce) skinless cod fillets, 2 inches thick
- Salt and pepper

Procedure

1. Toast guajillos in medium deep cooking pan on moderate heat, stirring regularly, until aromatic, 2 to six minutes; move to container.

2. Heat 1 tablespoon oil in now empty pot on moderate heat until it starts to shimmer Put in onion and cook until tender, approximately five minutes.

3. Mix in garlic, oregano, cumin seeds, cloves, and allspice, and cook until aromatic, approximately half a minute. Mix in masa harina and cook for a minute. Slowly whisk in clam broth, scraping up any browned bits and smoothing out any lumps.

4. Mix in tomatillos, cilantro sprigs, toasted chiles, 1/2 teaspoon salt, and 1/4 teaspoon pepper, bring to simmer, and cook until tomatillos start to tenderize, approximately 3 minutes.

5. Cautiously move mixture to blender and pulse until smooth, one to two minutes. Return to pot and cover to keep warm.

6. Adjust oven rack to middle position and heat oven to 425 degrees. Pat fish dry using paper towels and season both sides with salt and pepper. If using any tail end fillets, tuck tail under. Drizzle sugar uniformly over 1 side of fish.

7. Heat remaining 1 tablespoon oil in 12 inches ovensafe nonstick frying pan using high heat until just smoking. Put fillets in frying pan, sugar side down, and press lightly to make sure even contact with pan. Cook until browned, approximately 2 minutes.

8. Using 2 spatulas, flip fillets. Move frying pan to oven and roast fish until centers are just opaque and register 140 degrees, 5 to ten minutes.

9. Using potholders (frying pan handle will be hot), remove frying pan from oven. Move fish to serving platter or individual dishes.

10. Serve with sauce.

Stuffed Fish

Ingredients

- 2 cups finely chopped white onion
- 2 tablespoons butter
- 3 tablespoons finely chopped flat-leaf parsley
- 1/3 cup (85 ml) fresh lime juice
- 12 pounds tomatoes, finely chopped
- 2 tablespoons olive oil
- 2 ounces raw scallops
- 12 ounces raw shrimps, peeled and deveined
- Salt and pepper to taste
- 2 garlic cloves
- 1 small red snappers
- 3 tablespoons melted butter
- 2 ounces cooked crabmeat

Procedure

1. Have the fish cleaned, leaving the head and tail on. Have as much of the backbone removed as you can to make a good pocket for stuffing the fish without completely opening it up.

2. Crush the garlic and mix it to a paste with the salt, pepper, and lime juice. Prick the fish all over on both sides with a coarse-tined fork and rub the paste in well—inside and out. Set the fish aside to season for minimum 1 hour.

3. Preheat your oven to 350° f (180° c) and prepare the stuffing.

4. Melt the butter with the oil in a frying pan and cook the onion until translucent. Put in the tomatoes and cook them over quite high heat until some of the juice has vaporized.

5. Chop the shrimps into halves and the scallops into four equivalent portions. Put in them, with the parsley and seasoning, to the tomato mixture and allow to cook on moderate heat until the scallops and shrimps are just soft—about ten minutes. Mix in the crabmeat.

6. Stuff each fish with approximately 1/2 cup (125 ml) of the filling and sew it up. Put half of the butter into a shallow ovenproof dish, put the fish side by side, and drizzle them with the rest of the butter.

7. Cover the dish and bake until the fish are soft—about twenty minutes.

Fish Soup

Ingredients

- 1/4 cup vegetable oil
- 1/4 teaspoon dried mexican oregano
- 1/2 cup thinly cut white onion
- 2/3 cup loosely packed frutas en vinagre or an equivalent amount of sour pickles plus 2 slices lime
- 2 big sprigs cilantro, roughly chopped
- 4 cups chicken broth
- Salt and freshly ground pepper to taste
- 10 ounces cut tomatoes, approximately 2 cups
- 3 zucchini (about 6 ounces), slice into rounds
- 2 pounds whole catfish or carp
- 2 garlic cloves, left whole
- 2 jalapeño chiles en escabeche, roughly chopped
- 3 medium carrots (approximately four ounces), cut

Procedure

1. Wash and dry the fish well. Chop the body into 1-inch slices and the head, if used, into four pieces. Sprinkle with salt and freshly ground pepper.

2. Heat the oil in a large, heavy pan and fry the fish pieces very lightly; the flesh should just turn opaque. Remove and save for later.

3. In the same oil, fry the tomatoes, onion, and garlic together until the onion is tender and the mixture has a saucelike consistency.

4. Put in the broth, carrots, zucchini, oregano, chiles, and frutas en vinagre (or substitutes) to the pan and cook until the vegetables are just soft, approximately twenty minutes.

5. Put in the fish pieces and simmer until the flesh flakes easily from the bone—about ten minutes.

6. Take away the pan from the heat and put in the chopped cilantro. Serve the soup accompanied by freshly made tortillas.

Chilean Shrimps and Green Beans

Serves 3 pax

Ingredients

- 2 cups green beans, trimmed and slice into 1-inch lengths
- 3 teaspoons jalapeno sauce
- 1/2 cup cleaned shrimp
- 1 tablespoon Red chili Paste
- 1 tablespoon vegetable oil
- 2 teaspoons sugar

Procedure

1. Heat the vegetable oil on moderate heat. Mix in the chili paste and cook for a minute to release the fragrance.

2. Put in the shrimp and the green beans at the same time, and stir-fry until the shrimp become opaque. (The green beans will still be fairly crunchy. If you prefer your beans softer, cook an additional minute.)

3. Put in the jalapeno sauce and the sugar; stir until blended.

4. Serve instantly with rice.

Calamari Rice

Ingredients

- 1 tablespoon minced fresh oregano or 3/4 teaspoon dried
- 2 pounds extra big shrimp (21 to 25 per pound), peeled
- 2 bay leaves
- 1 (14.5 ounce) can diced tomatoes
- 1 green bell pepper, stemmed, seeded, and chopped
- 1 tablespoon black peppercorns
- 2 garlic cloves, minced
- 3 sprigs fresh cilantro plus 2 tablespoons minced
- 4 tablespoons extra virgin olive oil
- 5 Lime wedges
- 2 cups long grain white rice
- 2 onions, chopped
- 4 cups water
- 4 guajillo chiles, stemmed, seeded, and torn
- Pinch cayenne pepper

Procedure

1. Heat 1 tablespoon oil in big deep cooking pan on moderate heat. Put in shrimp shells, 1 cup onion, guajillos, and 1 teaspoon salt and cook, stirring once in a while, until shells are spotty brown, approximately ten minutes.

2. Put in water, peppercorns, cilantro sprigs, and bay leaves, increase heat to high, and bring to boiling point.

3. Decrease the heat to low, cover, and simmer for half an hour Strain shrimp stock through fine mesh strainer into big liquid measuring cup; you should have 3 cups stock. (If you have extra, reserve for future use.)

4. In the meantime, whisk 2 tablespoons oil, half of garlic, cayenne, and 1/2 teaspoon pepper together in big container.

5. Put in shrimp and toss to coat. Cover and place in your fridge for half an hour

6. Heat remaining 3 tablespoons oil in Dutch oven on moderate heat until it starts to shimmer.

7. Put in bell pepper, remaining onion, and 1/2 teaspoon salt and cook until vegetables start to tenderize, five to seven minutes.
8. Mix in rice, remaining garlic, and oregano and cook until aromatic and rice is translucent, approximately 2 minutes.
9. Mix in tomatoes and their juice and 3 cups shrimp stock. Bring to boil, then decrease the heat to low, cover, and cook for about twenty minutes.
10. Nestle shrimp attractively into rice, in concentric circles, with tails sticking up out of
11. rice. Cover and cook until shrimp are opaque, about eight to ten minutes. Remove pot from heat and allow it to sit, covered, until shrimp are thoroughly cooked, approximately five minutes.
12. Drizzle with minced cilantro and serve with lime wedges.

Capers Sauce Fish

Serves 6 pax

Ingredients

For the fish broth:

- 2 tablespoons fresh lime juice
- 4 cups water, or enough to just cover the fish
- 8 ounces carrots, scraped and thinly cut
- 8 ounces turnips, peeled and thinly cut
- A 3-pound striped bass or snook Salt to taste
- 1/3 cup thinly cut white onion
- 12 peppercorns
- 2 mexican bay leaves

For the sauce:

- 1 sprig flat-leaf parsley
- 1 tablespoon big capers, washed
- 1/4 cup roughly cut white onion
- 1/2 cup fresh breadcrumbs
- 1/2 cup olive oil

- 2 cups reserved fish broth
- 2 ounces blanched almonds, roughly chopped
- 6 big lettuce leaves, torn into pieces
- 2 garlic cloves
- Salt to taste

For the topping:

- 12 pitted green olives
- 6 ounces tomatoes, thinly cut
- 3/4 cup thinly cut white onion
- 1 tablespoon big capers, washed
- The heart of a romaine lettuce

Procedure

1. Put all the ingredients for the broth in a big deep cooking pan and simmer for approximately 30 minutes. Strain and set aside but keep warm.
2. Clean the fish, leaving the head and tail on, and put in a shallow flameproof baking dish.

3. Cover the fish with the warm broth and poach on top of the stove using low heat until just cooked—about twenty minutes. Pour off the broth and save for later.

4. Preheat your oven to 350° f (180° c).

5. In a coffee/spice grinder, grind the almonds as fine as you can—this should make about 1/2 cup.

6. Put 1 cup of the reserved broth into a blender jar, put in the ground almonds, breadcrumbs, lettuce leaves, capers, parsley, 2 garlic cloves, and the onion, and blend to a slightly textured sauce. Set aside.

7. Heat the oil gently, put in the remaining 2 garlic cloves, and the moment they start to brown, remove using a slotted spoon and discard.

8. Mix in the mixed sauce, put in 1/2 cup reserved broth, and cook using low heat until well seasoned—approximately eight minutes.

9. Pour the sauce over the fish and put into the oven until thoroughly heated—about fifteen minutes.

10. Place the lettuce leaves around the dish and top with the remaining ingredients.

Broiled Achiote Fish

Ingredients

- 1/4 cup olive oil
- 2 groupers or red snappers, 2 pounds each
- 1/4 cup seville orange juice or mild white vinegar
- 1 tablespoon achiote seeds, crushed
- 3 garlic cloves, roughly chopped
- 1/4 teaspoon dried mexican oregano, toasted
- 3 Sliced seville oranges
- 3 Sliced tomatoes
- Toasted mexican oregano
- 1/4 teaspoon peppercorns, crushed
- 1/4 teaspoon powdered chile seco or árbol
- Salt to taste
- 2 Habanero chiles, chopped
- 3 Pickled Onions, chopped
- 3 Sliced avocado

Procedure

1. *Do not have the scales removed from the fish.* Have the heads and tails removed and the fish opened out flat in one piece. Take away the backbone.

2. Grind and blend all the ingredients for the seasoning paste to a smooth consistency. Spread the paste, not too thickly, over the flesh (opened side of the fish) and set aside to season for approximately 2 hours.

3. Brush the seasoned side of the fish with the oil and cook it, seasoned side down, over the charcoal or under the broiler for five to 8 minutes.

4. Turn the fish over and cook it on the skin side for a slightly longer period or until flesh is just thoroughly cooked— about fifteen minutes, depending on the thickness of the fish.

5. Serve hot with fresh tortillas.

Mackerel, Fennel and Orange Salad

Serves 4 pax

Ingredients

- 4 smoked mackerel filets
- Juice of $1/2$ lemon
- 1 cup Olive oil
- 1 bulb fennel
- 2 blood oranges, peeled, pith removed
- 2 handfuls of shaved Parmesan cheese

Procedure

1. Remove any tough stalks from the fennel. Finely chop a few of the feathery leaves and reserve. Thinly slice the fennel and spread it out on a large plate.
2. Now cut the blood orange into segments and remove all the membranes. Spread the segments evenly over the fennel.
3. Drizzle the lemon juice on top, then lightly drizzle on some olive oil.
4. Top it all off with some shaved Parmesan, mackerel and the chopped fennel leaves.

Cilantro Fish

Ingredients

- 1 scant teaspoon salt
- 2 cups thinly cut white onions
- 1/3 cup fresh lime juice
- 3 pounds red snapper
- Freshly ground pepper
- 1/3 cup olive oil
- 2 cups roughly chopped cilantro
- 3 jalapeño chiles en escabeche
- 2 tablespoons juice from the chile can

Procedure

1. Have the fish cleaned, leaving the head and tail on.
2. Prick the fish well on both sides with a coarse-tined fork and rub it with the salt and pepper. Put the fish onto a baking dish with half the onions underneath and the rest on top.
3. Pour the lime juice over it and set it aside for approximately 1 hour, flipping it over once during that time.
4. Preheat your oven to 350° f.
5. Cover the dish and bake the fish for approximately fifteen minutes on each side.
6. Put in the remaining ingredients and carry on cooking the fish, covered, until it is just cooked, coating it occasionally with the juices in the dish— about twenty minutes.

Paraguay Fish

Ingredients

- 1 (14.5 ounce) can diced tomatoes, drained
- 1 onion, halved and cut thin
- 1 teaspoon chili powder
- 1/2 cup dry white wine
- 1/2 teaspoon ground cumin
- 4 (6 to 8 ounce) skinless cod fillets, one to 11/2 inches thick
- 2 garlic cloves, minced
- Salt and pepper
- 1 teaspoon minced fresh thyme or 1/4 teaspoon dried
- 3 tablespoons extra virgin olive oil, plus extra for serving
- 2 tablespoons minced fresh cilantro

Procedure

1. Heat oil in 12 inches nonstick frying pan over moderate high heat until it starts to shimmer Put in onion and 1/2 teaspoon salt and cook until tender, approximately five minutes.

2. Mix in garlic, chili powder, and cumin and cook until aromatic, approximately half a minute. Mix in tomatoes, wine, and thyme and bring to simmer.

3. Season cod with salt and pepper. If using any tail end fillets, tuck tail under. Nestle cod into frying pan and spoon some sauce over fish.

4. Cover, decrease the heat to moderate low, and cook until fish flakes apart when gently prodded with paring knife and records 140 degrees, approximately ten minutes.

5. Move fish to separate plates. Stir cilantro into sauce and sprinkle with salt and pepper to taste. Ladle sauce over fish and sprinkle with extra oil before you serve.

Garlic Charred Fish

Ingredients

- 1/3 cup plus 2 tablespoons olive oil
- 2 cups thickly cut white onions
- 2 tablespoons bitter orange juice or fruity vinegar
- 12 ounces tomatoes, thinly cut
- 1 big green bell pepper, thinly cut
- 1 heaped tablespoon dried mexican oregano
- 1 heaped tablespoon recado de toda clase
- 1 small bunch flat-leaf parsley, roughly chopped
- 2 güero chiles, charred and left whole
- A fish head, approximately 12 ounces
- Salt to taste
- 2 garlic cloves, roughly chopped
- 3 small heads garlic, well charred and cut in half
- 3 tablespoons fresh lime juice
- 6 fish steaks about 3/4 inch thick

Procedure

1. Flavor the fish, including the head, with the lime juice and salt and set aside for approximately fifteen minutes.

2. In a small container crush the garlic with the recado (or any other tastemaker of choice) and dilute with the orange juice. Spread a thin coating over the fish (and head) and set aside to season for minimum 1 hour.

3. Preheat your oven to 350° f.

4. Heat the 1/3 cup olive oil in a frying pan, put in the onions and bell pepper with a drizzling of salt, and fry using low heat until wilted, approximately 2 minutes.

5. Put in the tomato slices and carry on frying until some of the juice has vaporized— about three minutes.

6. Put one half of the tomato mixture in an ovenproof dish into which the fish and head will fit in a single layer, drizzle with half of the parsley, and cover with the remaining tomato mixture.

7. Put the garlic halves and chiles on the surface and drizzle with the oregano and the rest of the 2 tablespoons olive oil.

8. Cover the dish and bake for approximately twenty minutes. Take out of the oven and coat well with the juices, then cover and bake for 20 more minutes or until barely cooked.

9. Set aside to season for approximately 1/2 hour before you serve and then

10. reheat gently to avoid overcooking the fish.

Swordfish Sour Skewers

Ingredients

- 1 (2 pounds) skinless swordfish steak, cut
- 1 big red onion, cut into an inch pieces, 3 layers thick
- 1 teaspoon sugar
- 2 teaspoons minced shallot
- 4 tablespoons extra virgin olive oil
- 1 tablespoon ground coriander
- 1 teaspoon ground cumin
- Salt and pepper
- 4 tablespoons chopped fresh cilantro
- 2 limes, halved, then each half quartered

Procedure

1. Lightly toss onion with 1 tablespoon oil in container, cover, and microwave until just

2. soft, approximately 2 minutes. Mix 2 tablespoons oil, coriander, cumin, sugar, 1/2 teaspoon salt, and 1/2 teaspoon pepper in big container.

3. Pat fish dry using paper towels, put into spice mixture, and toss lightly to coat. Thread fish, limes, and onion uniformly onto four 12 inches metal skewers, in alternating pattern.

4. FOR A GAS GRILL: Set all burners to high, cover, and heat grill until hot, approximately fifteen minutes. Turn all burners to moderate high.

5. Clean cooking grate, then constantly brush grate with well-oiled paper towels until black and shiny, five to ten times. Put skewers on grill.

6. Cook (covered if using gas), turning as required, until fish appears opaque and flakes apart when gently prodded with paring knife, 5 to 8 minutes.

7. Move skewers to platter, tent loosely with aluminium foil, and allow to rest for five minutes.
8. Mix remaining 2 tablespoons oil, cilantro, and shallot in container and sprinkle with salt and pepper to taste.
9. Brush skewers with oil mixture before you serve.

Grilled Red Snapper and Chilean Vinaigrette

Ingredients

- 1 garlic clove, minced
- 1 tablespoon chopped fresh cilantro
- 1/4 cup orange juice
- 1/2 cup plus 1 tablespoon extra-virgin olive oil
- 1 tablespoon lime juice, plus lime wedges for serving
- 4 (1 pound) whole red snapper, scaled and gutted
- 2 teaspoons sugar
- Salt and pepper

Procedure

1. Whisk orange juice, lime juice, sugar, garlic, 1/2 teaspoon salt, and 1/4 teaspoon pepper together in medium container, then whisk in 6 tablespoons oil.

2. Whisk in cilantro and sprinkle with salt and pepper to taste. Pat snapper dry using paper towels. Using sharp knife, make shallow diagonal slashes an inch apart through skin on both sides of fish, being cautious not to cut into flesh.

3. Rub fish with remaining 3 tablespoons oil, then season meticulously (including cavities) with salt and pepper.

4. FOR A GAS GRILL: Set all burners to high, cover, and heat grill until hot, approximately fifteen minutes. Leave all burners on high.

5. Clean cooking grate, then constantly brush grate with well-oiled paper towels until black and shiny, five to ten times.

6. Put fish on grill. Cook (covered if using gas) until both sides are browned and crisp and flesh is no longer translucent in center, twelve to 16 minutes, softly turning fish over, using 2 spatulas midway through grilling. Move to carving board.
7. Working with 1 fish at a time, softly cut through skin and flesh down back of fish, from head to tail, without cutting through bones.
8. Lightly cut through skin and flesh just behind head, from top to bottom, without cutting through bones.
9. Beginning at head and working toward tail, slowly run metal spatula between bones and flesh to separate, then softly lift whole fillet from skeleton in single piece. Repeat on second side of fish.
10. Sprinkle fish with vinaigrette and serve with lime wedges.

Drunk Trout

Ingredients

- 1 garlic clove
- 1 tablespoon plus 1/2 teaspoon sugar
- 1/3 cup orange juice
- 1/2 teaspoon ground coriander
- 3 tablespoons lime juice, plus lime wedges for serving
- 4 dried pasilla chiles, stemmed, seeded, and torn
- 4 (6 to 8 ounce) trout fillets, 1/4 to 1/2 inch thick
- 2 tablespoons extra virgin olive oil scallions, white parts chopped, green parts cut thin
- 4 tablespoons tequila
- Salt and pepper

Procedure

1. Toast pasillas in small deep cooking pan on moderate heat, stirring regularly, until aromatic, 2 to six minutes; move to blender.

2. Put in orange juice, tequila, scallion whites, 3 tablespoons oil, 1 tablespoon sugar, garlic, coriander, and 1/4 teaspoon salt to blender and pulse until smooth, approximately one minute.

3. Return sauce to now empty pot and simmer on moderate heat, stirring frequently, until slightly thickened, 2 to 4 minutes. Turn off the heat; cover to keep warm.

4. In the meantime, pat fish dry using paper towels and season both sides with salt and pepper. Drizzle remaining 1/2 teaspoon sugar uniformly over 1 side of fish.

5. Heat 1 tablespoon oil in 12 inches nonstick frying pan using high heat until it starts to shimmer Lay half of fish in frying pan, sugar side down, and press lightly to make sure even contact with pan.

6. Cook until edges of fillets are opaque and bottoms are mildly browned, two to three minutes. Using 2 spatulas, flip fillets.

7. Cook on second side until thickest part of fillets is firm to touch and fish flakes easily, two to three minutes.

8. Move fish to platter and tent with aluminium foil. Repeat with 1 tablespoon oil and remaining fish.

9. Stir lime juice and remaining 1 tablespoon oil into sauce and sprinkle with salt and

10. pepper to taste. Move fish to individual serving plates, leaving any collected juices behind on platter.

11. Ladle small amount of sauce over fish and drizzle with scallion greens.

12. Serve with rest of the sauce and lime wedges.

Kali Shredded Fish

Ingredients

- 1/4 teaspoon coriander seeds, crushed
- 6 ounces tomatoes, finely chopped
- 1/2 teaspoon salt, or to taste
- 1/2-inch piece of cinnamon stick, crushed
- 1/4 cup finely chopped white onion
- 1/4 cup water
- 1 small ancho chile
- 2 serrano chiles, or any fresh, finely chopped
- 4 tablespoons light olive oil
- 1 teaspoon capers, washed, strained and chopped
- 2 tablespoons raisins
- 12 peppercorns, crushed
- 2 cups (cooked and firm-fleshed shredded fish
- 2 garlic cloves
- 6 green olives, pitted and finely chopped

Procedure

1. Take away the seeds and veins from the ancho chile, cover with water, and simmer for five minutes. Soak for another five minutes, then drain and put into the blender jar.

2. Put in the crushed spices, salt, garlic, and water and blend, putting in more water only if required, to a loose paste.

3. Heat the oil in a heavy frying pan and fry the paste for approximately one minute. Put in the tomatoes, onion, serrano chiles, olives, capers, and raisins.

4. Fry on moderate heat for approximately five minutes, stirring occasionally, for approximately five minutes. Mix in the shredded fish and cook for five minutes longer.

5. Tweak the seasoning and serve either hot or cold, with freshly made tortillas.

Clams and Chorizo

Ingredients

- 1 onion, chopped fine
- 1 tablespoon vegetable oil
- 1 (28 ounce) can diced tomatoes
- 2 pounds littleneck clams, scrubbed
- 4 ounces Mexican style chorizo sausage, casings remove
- 1 cup beer
- 2 serrano chiles, stemmed and cut thin
- 3 tablespoons minced fresh cilantro
- 2 garlic cloves, minced
- 4 Lime wedges

Procedure

1. Heat oil in Dutch oven on moderate heat until it starts to shimmer Put in chorizo and cook, breaking into 1/2 inch pieces with wooden spoon, until starting to brown, approximately five minutes. Move chorizo to paper towel–lined plate, leaving fat in pot. Put in onion to fat left in pot and cook over moderate high heat until tender, five to seven minutes.

2. Mix in serranos and garlic and cook until aromatic, approximately half a minute. Mix in tomatoes and their juice and beer.

3. Decrease the heat to moderate and simmer until slightly thickened, about eight to ten minutes.

4. Increase heat to high and mix in clams and reserved chorizo. Cover and cook, stirring once, until clams have opened, four to 8 minutes.

5. Using slotted spoon, move clams to serving container or individual bowls; discard any clams that haven't opened. Stir cilantro into broth, then pour broth over clams.

6. Serve with lime wedges.

Clams Linguini

Ingredients

- 2 garlic cloves, chopped
- 1/4 cup extra-virgin olive oil
- 6 red bell peppers
- 1 shallot, chopped
- 20 pounds clams
- 1/2 cup parsley, chopped
- 1/2 cup white wine
- 1/4 teaspoon chile flakes
- 2 tomatoes, chopped
- 10 pounds linguine

Procedure

1. Scrub and rinse clams. Preheat broiler.
2. Halve peppers long ways. Remove seeds and ribs. Broil skin side up until skins char.
3. Freeze roasted peppers 10 minutes to loosen skins. Rub off blackened skins. Chop skinned peppers and set aside.
4. Boil a large pot of salted water.
5. Heat oil in large skillet on medium-high heat.
6. Add shallot and garlic. Sauté 3 minutes until soft. Add wine. Cook 1 minute. Stir in chile and tomatoes. Cook 2 minutes.
7. Put linguine in boiling water. Cook 5 minutes.
8. Add clams to garlic and pepper mix.
9. Raise to high heat. Cover skillet and cook 5 minutes. Drain pasta and add to clams skillet. Cover and cook 5 minutes more. Stir intermittently.
10. Dish is done when clams open and pasta is al dente. Remove and discard unopened clams. Transfer to large bowl. Sprinkle with parsley.
11. Toss pasta and clams with parsley until well mixed.
12. Serve hot.

Chilean Noodles

Ingredients

- 1–2 teaspoons red pepper flakes
- 4 cups cooked shrimps in bite-sized pieces
- 1 green onions, trimmed and thinly cut
- 1/4 cup chili sauce
- 1 package rice sticks, soaked in hot water until tender and drained
- 3 tablespoons chili powder
- 3 cloves garlic, minced
- 2 tablespoons minced ginger
- 2 tablespoons vegetable oil
- 3 teaspoons cilantro sauce

Procedure

1. Heat the vegetable oil in a wok or big frying pan on moderate to high heat. Put in the garlic and the ginger. Stir-fry until tender.
2. Put in the cooked shrimps, green onion, and red pepper flakes to the wok; stir-fry until hot.
3. Mix in the chili sauce, chili powder, and cilantro sauce. Put in the rice noodles and toss.
4. Serve instantly.

Tilapia in Parsley Coat

Serves 6 pax

Ingredients

- 2 cups breadcrumbs.
- 4 tablespoons fresh parsley, chopped fine
- 7 tablespoons extra-virgin olive oil
- 6 tilapia fillets.
- 4 eggs
- 2 cups all-purpose flour
- Salt
- Freshly grounded black pepper

Procedure

1. Season tilapia fillets with salt and pepper to taste. Let sit 15 minutes.
2. Whisk eggs in medium bowl. Combine flour, salt and pepper to taste. Spread in shallow dish.
3. Combine breadcrumbs, chopped parsley, salt and pepper to taste. Spread in second shallow dish.
4. Coat fillet both sides with flour mixture. Dip coated fillet in egg.
5. Press coated fillet into breadcrumbs. Lightly press both sides.
6. Repeat process until all fillets are coated.
7. Heat oil in large skillet on low heat. Place fillets carefully into skillet. Sauté until golden brown both sides.

Shrimps Noodles

Ingredients

- 1 tablespoon soy or fish sauce
- Sesame oil to taste
- 1 tablespoon vegetable oil
- 1 teaspoon sugar
- 2 cloves garlic, chopped
- 1/4 cup chopped cilantro
- 7 ounces package rice noodles
- 1 medium onion, thinly cut
- 30 black peppercorns
- 6 big shrimp, shell on, washed and patted dry

Procedure

1. Soak the noodles in hot water until soft, approximately ten minutes. Drain and save for later.

2. Using a mortar and pestle or a food processor, meticulously mix the garlic, cilantro, and peppercorns.

3. Put in the vegetable oil to a wok or big frying pan using low heat. Put in the garlic mixture and stir-fry for a minute. Put in the cut onion and carry on cooking until the onion is soft, then remove the heat.

4. Put in the sugar, soy sauce, and a few drops of sesame oil to the wok; stir until blended. Put in the noodles and toss to coat.

5. Pour the noodle mixture into an ovenproof baking dish. Put the whole shrimp on top of the noodles, cover the dish, and bake for about twenty minutes in a 400-degree oven.

6. Serve instantly.

Avocado, Seafood and Sour Vinaigrette

Ingredients

- 1/4 teaspoon paprika
- 3 cups cider vinegar
- 2 cups crab, cooked and flaked
- 2 cups shrimp, cooked
- 6 tablespoons cucumber, diced
- 3 tablespoons fresh cilantro,
- Salt and freshly grounded black pepper
- 1/4 cup olive oil
- 1 teaspoon lime zest
- 2 tablespoons lime juice
- 1 tablespoon honey

Procedure

1. Mix crab, shrimp and cucumber in bowl. Season to taste with salt and pepper. Cover and refrigerate until chilled.
2. Halve each avocado lengthwise and remove the stone. Scoop out middle of each half. Leave 1/2" of avocado on the skin.
3. Spoon the chilled seafood into scooped avocado shells. Sprinkle tops with paprika.
4. Whisk vinegar, cilantro, lime zest, lime juice, honey and 1/4 teaspoon salt in bowl.
5. Slowly add in oil while continuing to whisk.
6. When mixed smooth and well whisked, drizzle over avocado boats.
7. Serve immediately.

Thank you, *dear fish lover.*

I am glad you accepted my teachings.

These meals have been personally codified in my worldwide trips.

I wanted to share them with you, to let people know more about meat and how to treat it properly.

Now you had come to know about South American fish in all of its shapes, let me give you one more tip.

This manual takes part of an unmissable cookbooks collection.

These fish-based recipes, mixed to all the tastes I met around the world, will give you a complete idea of the possibilities this world offers to us.

You have now the opportunity to add hundreds new elements to your cooking skills knowledge.

Check out the other books!

Ernest Pescara

CPSIA information can be obtained
at www.ICGtesting.com
Printed in the USA
BVHW042132080621
609011BV00012B/2563